Y0-DOI-170

DATE DUE			

DOLPHINS

Dolphin Magic for Kids

To Anne, Jennifer, Andy, Nick, Jaclyn, Katie, and Rachel –
and all kids who love dolphins.

– Patricia Corrigan

For a free color catalog describing Gareth Stevens' list of high-quality books, call 1-800-542-2595 (USA) or 1-800-461-9120 (Canada). Gareth Stevens' Fax: 414-225-0377.

Library of Congress Cataloging-in-Publication Data

Corrigan, Patricia, 1948-
    Dolphin magic for kids / by Patricia Corrigan ; photography by Flip Nicklin ; illustrated by John F. McGee.
       p. cm. — (Animal magic for kids)
    "Based on the book Dolphins for kids . . . by Patricia Corrigan" — T.p. verso.
    Includes index.
    Summary: Explores the physical characteristics, behavior, life cycle, and personalities of these popular sea creatures.
    ISBN-0-8368-1374-X
    1. Dolphins—Juvenile literature. [1. Dolphins.] I. Nicklin, Flip, ill. II. McGee, John F., ill. III. Title. IV. Title: Dolphins. V. Series.
    QL737.C432C585   1995
    599.5'3—dc20   95-16625

This edition first published in 1995 by
Gareth Stevens Publishing
1555 North RiverCenter Drive, Suite 201
Milwaukee, Wisconsin 53212 USA

Based on the book, *Dolphins for Kids*, text © 1995 by Patricia Corrigan, all photographs © 1995 by Flip Nicklin/Minden Pictures except pp. 44-45, © Sam Abell/National Geographic Society, with illustrations by John F. McGee. First published in the United States in 1995 by NorthWord Press, Inc., Minocqua, Wisconsin. End matter © 1995 by Gareth Stevens, Inc.

All rights to this edition reserved to Gareth Stevens, Inc. No part of this book may be reproduced, stored in a retrieval system or transmitted in any form or by any means, electronic, mechanical, photocopying, recording, or otherwise without the prior written permission of the publisher except for the inclusion of brief quotations in an acknowledged review.

Printed in the United States of America

1 2 3 4 5 6 7 8 9 99 98 97 96 95

by Patricia Corrigan
photography by Flip Nicklin

DOLPHINS

Dolphin Magic for Kids

Gareth Stevens Publishing
MILWAUKEE

A dolphin is smiling at me! Right away, my face stretches into a big grin and I smile back.

This particular dolphin smiles at me from the cover of a magazine lying on a table here at the library. I'm waiting for my mom to pick me up. The last thing I expected to see was a dolphin.

My name is Katie. I'm 10. Luckily, I know about dolphins.

Some people are surprised to learn that dolphins are mammals, just like us. Mammals are warm-blooded, we give birth to our young instead of laying eggs, and we breathe air. Because dolphins live in water, they must come to the surface to breathe. There, they quickly release almost all the breath they've been holding and they take in a big new breath. Then they close up a little breathing hole on the top of their head, called a blowhole, and they dive again.

Imagine living your whole life underwater, holding your breath, and popping up for air every few minutes!

Bottlenose Dolphin

Dolphins are related to whales and porpoises. They all are part of one big group, or order, called cetacea. (That's pronounced "SEE-TAY-SHA.") Some people call all 77 species of cetaceans "whales." Others divide them into three groups: 32 species of whales, 39 of dolphins, and 6 of porpoises. Some dolphins have the name "whale," but scientists consider them dolphins because of their physical characteristics.

I know all this because my teacher, Mrs. Gwyn, invited Miss Currens to class one day to talk to us. She had curly red hair, and she wore a purple dress with a navy blue vest. The vest had little cloth dolphins sewn on it. She showed us her necklace, too. It had charms on it, in the shapes of dolphins, whales, turtles, and even a seahorse.

We saw slides of some of the different cetaceans. There are solid-color dolphins, dolphins with patches of color, striped dolphins, and spotted dolphins.

Some dolphins' names describe how they look. Some are named for the scientist who first studied them. And some of the names are in the language of the country where the dolphins live.

For instance, the white dolphin is called a beluga, or white whale, because of its white skin. It has another name, too—canary of the sea. That's because belugas chirp and squeal all the time, underwater as well as above. They live in the far north, in the Arctic region.

Beluga

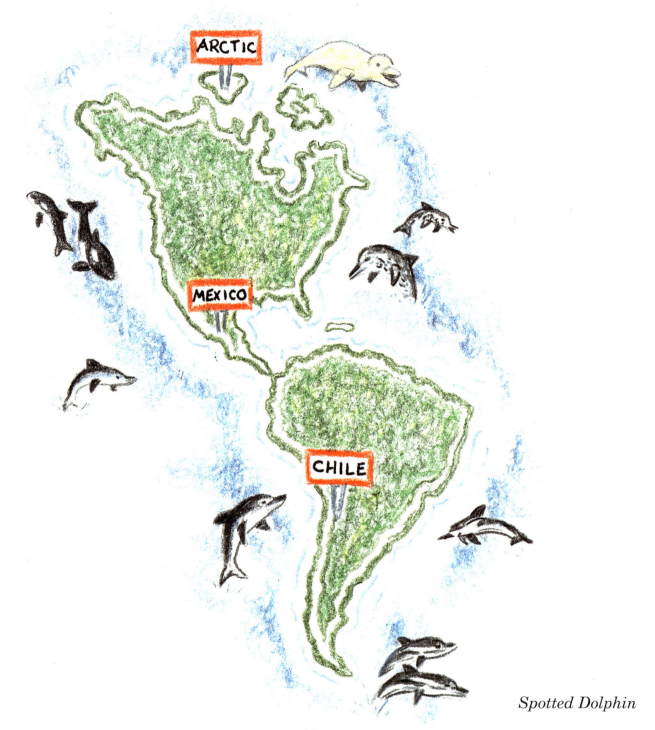

ARCTIC

MEXICO

CHILE

Spotted Dolphin

The black dolphin isn't really black, but has a dark gray body with a white throat and belly. Black dolphins live off the coast of Chile.

Miss Currens said you can tell how old a spotted dolphin is by how many spots it has. The babies are born with just a few, she said, and the older animals have lots and lots of spots—hundreds!

Spotted dolphins live in oceans all over the world. Striped dolphins have two black stripes. They both begin at the dolphin's eye. One stripe runs down to its flipper, and one runs the whole length of the dolphin. They also live in oceans all over the world.

Most dolphins' bodies look a lot alike. They are sleek and stream-lined, designed to propel the animals through the water as fast as 25 miles per hour.

All dolphins have flippers, just about where we have arms. Their tails are called flukes. Most dolphins also have a fin on their backs, called a dorsal fin. Dorsal fins come in different shapes and sizes.

Also, some dolphins have long snouts, called beaks.

Some porpoises look like dolphins, but porpoises usually have smaller heads, with no snout, and small blunt teeth. Dolphins' teeth are sharp and pointed.

One dolphin, the narwhal ("NAR-WAL"), has unusual teeth. Adult narwhals have just two teeth, and one of them grows into a tusk almost 10 feet long! That's about two thirds the length of the narwhal itself. The tusk spirals right out of the dolphin's upper gum, and it can weigh as much as 20 pounds.

Miss Currens said narwhals sometimes fight each other with their tusks, as though they were swords. Narwhals live in the Arctic.

Narwhal

Dolphins and porpoises come in many sizes. One of the smaller dolphins is Hector's dolphin, which was named after the scientist in New Zealand who first studied it.

An adult Hector's dolphin grows to just over 5 feet and weighs about 125 pounds. A porpoise called the vaquita ("VA-KEE-TA"), which means "little cow" in Spanish, is even smaller. Some vaquitas are only about four feet long.

I'm taller than that already, but I don't weigh as much as a vaquita, which can grow to 100 pounds or more.

Vaquitas live off the coast of Mexico.

Hector's Dolphin

If you've seen the movie *Free Willy*, then you've seen the biggest dolphin. Willy is an orca, or killer whale. The name "killer whale" makes some people think that orcas are whales, but I know they're dolphins.

I also know that a long time ago, some whalers called orcas "whale killers," because some orcas do hunt other whales. Over the years, the words somehow got reversed. I prefer to say "orca," rather than "killer whale." Orca means "a kind of whale" in Latin.

Orcas have tall dorsal fins that stick straight up out of the water, and their skin is shiny black and white. They remind me a little bit of some old shoes in Dad's closet that he calls "saddle shoes."

Orca

Orcas grow as long as 30 feet, and they weigh as much as ten tons—that's 20,000 pounds, or about twice as much as a male Asian elephant! Most orcas spend all their time with their families. The family groups, called pods, swim as far as 100 miles a day.

Orcas eat fish, especially big fish, such as salmon, but they also hunt seals, sharks, birds, and turtles. An adult orca eats about 400 pounds of food a day.

Miss Currens said that smaller dolphins eat fish and other small sea creatures. You and I can't eat underwater, but dolphins can. That's because they don't breathe through their mouths, as we do, but through that blowhole on top of their head. The blowhole is always closed when dolphins are underwater, and that's how they can open their mouths and eat a fish or squid without taking water into their lungs and drowning.

Dolphins also have a special navigation system, called echolocation ("EKO-LO-KAY-SHUN"). Here's how it works: Dolphins make clicking and whistling sounds. The waves from those sounds bounce back off other creatures or objects in the water. When the sound waves return, the dolphin feels a vibration in its jawbone, all the way back to its ear. That way, dolphins "hear" what's ahead, how far away it is and how big it is. Echolocation helps dolphins find food and figure out where they are going when they swim.

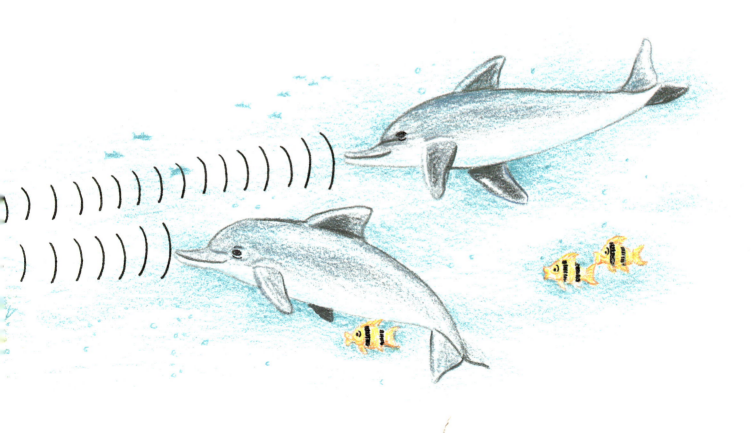

I've never seen dolphins swimming, but I know someone who has. Mr. Winter, my friend Christa's grandfather, is a fisherman in Florida. Last year when he came to visit Christa, he took us out for ice cream. He told us how he'd be out on the ocean in his boat, fishing and minding his own business, and suddenly dozens of dolphins would show up.

Usually, he said, they were bottlenose dolphins, which are commonly seen in most oceans. (That's not to confuse them with another dolphin called the common dolphin, which is also found in most oceans.)

He says they look as if they are playing in the wake, or waves, the boat makes. The dolphins dive and jump and dart back and forth in the water. Mr. Winter said he hears them "talking," whistling, and clicking. No one knows exactly how dolphins communicate with each other, but scientists say those sounds are different from the clicks and whistles that dolphins make for echolocation.

Most people think dolphins are smart. Many dolphins have big brains, about the same size as gorillas' brains. In captivity, dolphins quickly learn to jump up out of the water when their trainers tell them to. Mr. Winter told us that dolphins also jump all the way out of the water out in the ocean, where their bodies sparkle for a few seconds in the sun. It looks like fun, he said.

Maybe that's why dolphins are always smiling. Of course, we don't know whether they are happy or having fun, because their mouths just curve that way. Dolphins looked like that 50 million years ago, and dolphins look like that today.

Mr. Winter told us a description of dolphins he read in a book by a man named Herman Melville. I remember what he said—that dolphins on the sea "keep tossing themselves to heaven like caps in a Fourth-of-July crowd."

Mr. Winter says that sums it up nicely.

Most dolphins live in oceans, but five species live in rivers. One river dolphin, the franciscana ("FRAN-SES-KAY-NA"), has been seen in rivers and salt water, too. The tucuxi ("TOO-KOOK-SEE"), a coastal dolphin, also ventures into rivers. I guess they can't decide!

I live by a river, but it's the wrong river, as far as dolphins go. None of the five species of river dolphins live in U.S. rivers.

Miss Currens said the dolphins that live in the rivers in India have tiny eyes and are nearly blind. That's okay, because the water is too murky to see in, anyway. Like other dolphins, they use their echolocation to navigate and find food.

Boutu Dolphin

A boy in my class told a really neat story about the pink dolphins, called boutu ("BOO-TOO"), that live in the Amazon River.

Jorge said his cousin, who lived in Peru for awhile, told him how the pink dolphins come out of the river at night, turn into people and go dancing. The dolphin people always have red hair, just like Miss Currens. They always wear hats to hide their blowholes, which are still on the top of their heads even though they look like people.

It would be fun to meet a red-haired person who was a dolphin, but I think it's just a legend.

I know another legend, too. In ancient Greece, people believed that dolphins saved sailors lost at sea during shipwrecks. A dolphin would swim by and the sailor would grab the dolphin's dorsal fin. Then the dolphin would swim to shore, towing the sailor. My mom told me that story the day we put new candles in the dolphin candle holders on our dining room table.

Whether they live in rivers, along coasts, or in oceans, all dolphins face risks. Factories dump chemicals in rivers and oceans that are poisonous to dolphins. In some parts of the world, dolphins have sores on their bodies from the poisons.

Some dolphins get trapped and drown in huge nets that float in the oceans. The nets are meant for fish, but they catch dolphins too. In some countries, people catch and eat dolphins, just as though they were fish. And sometimes, whole pods of dolphins swim ashore and die on the beach. That's called a "stranding." Scientists can't say for sure why stranding happens.

Scientists also aren't certain why some dolphins spend their whole lives in one place. My dad showed me an article in the newspaper about a bottlenose dolphin named Funghie that lives off the southwest coast of Ireland.

Funghie has lived in the same waters since 1984. He swims into Dingle Harbor every day to greet the fishing boats going out to sea.

Some of the fishermen in Dingle also take dolphin watchers out in boats to meet Funghie, the article said.

I hope I can meet Funghie someday, too!

Funghie the dolphin

GLOSSARY

Beluga: A type of dolphin that becomes white as an adult (page 10).

Blowhole: A nostril on the top of a dolphin or other cetacean (page 6).

Captivity: The condition of being kept in confinement or under the control of another (page 37).

Cetacean: A member of an order of aquatic, mostly marine, mammals that includes whales, dolphins, and porpoises (page 9).

Dorsal: Near the back or on the back (page 15).

Echolocation: A process whereby an animal locates objects by using sound waves that are reflected back to the animal (page 29).

Flipper: A wide, flat limb on an animal that is used for swimming (page 13).

Legend: A story handed down from earlier times (page 41).

Narwhal: An arctic cetacean; a male narwhal has a long, twisted tusk (page 16).

Navigation: The act of directing the course of something or someone (page 29).

Order: A group of animals or plants whose members are similar in many ways (page 9).

Pod: A group of animals like dolphins or whales clustered together (page 26).

Stranding: The beaching of a whale or other animal (page 42).

Tusk: A long, pointed tooth that projects outside the closed mouth of an animal (page 16).

Wake (n): The track or path of waves left in the water by a moving boat or other object (page 32).

ADULT-CHILD INTERACTION QUESTIONS

These are questions designed to encourage young readers to participate in further study and discussion of dolphins.

1. Use an atlas or globe to find the places where the dolphins featured in this book live.

2. How are dolphins and porpoises different? How are they alike?

3. Why aren't there dolphins living in the rivers of the United States?

4. Does the narwhal use its tusk for other purposes besides self defense?

5. Make a list of the adaptations dolphins have to help them survive in the water.

6. How are dolphins like whales? How are they different?

7. What messages do you think dolphins are sending when they whistle or click to one another?

8. How many orcas, or killer whales, can be found living in a pod, or family unit?

9. Do you think it would be fun to be a dolphin?

10. Can you think of any other animals that use echolocation?

MORE BOOKS TO READ

A Closer Look at Whales and Dolphins by Elizabeth Strachan (Franklin Watts)
Dolphins by The Cousteau Society (Simon & Schuster)
Dolphins: Our Friends in the Sea by Donald Crump (National Geographic Society)
Killer Whales and Dolphin Play by Don Torgersen (Childrens)
Nine True Dolphin Stories by Margaret Davidson (Hastings)
Whales and Dolphins by Francene Sabin (Troll)

VIDEOS

Dolphin (Media Guild)
Dolphins and Whales (Barr Films)